ELIZABETH GOODWIN

Copyright © 2014 Elizabeth Goodwin

All rights reserved. No part of this book may be used or reproduced by any means, graphic, electronic, or mechanical, including photocopying, recording, taping or by any information storage retrieval system without the written permission of the copyright owner except in the case of brief quotations embodied in critical articles and reviews.

Design and layout by Katie Pelosi.

Serenity Press books may be ordered through online booksellers or by contacting:

Serenity Press
www.serenitypress.org
serenitypress@hotmail.com

Because of the dynamic nature of the Internet, any web addresses or links contained in this book may have changed since publication and may no longer be valid. The views expressed in this work are solely those of the authors and do not necessarily reflect the views of the publisher and the publisher hereby disclaims any responsibility for them.

The author of this book does not dispense medical advice or prescribe the use of any technique as a form of treatment for physical, emotional, or medical problems without the advice of a physician, either directly or indirectly. The intent of the author(s) is only to offer information of a general nature to help you in your quest for emotional and spiritual well-being and expression. In the event you use any of the information in this book for yourself, which is your constitutional right, the author(s) and the publisher assume no responsibility for your actions.

ISBN: (sc) 978-0-9924628-8-8
ISBN: (e) 978-0-9924628-9-5

CONTENTS

Who is your ideal partner?	1
Writing Goals	3
Getting honest with yourself	9
Step 1: Get the Feel	15
Step 2: Get the Look	25
Step 3: Character Traits	33
Step 4: Get the Experience	43
Final Note	59
About The Author	62

♥
INTRODUCTION

Who is your ideal partner?

Introduction

Have you ever sat down and thought about what you really want in a relationship? Do you know what your perfect relationship would look like, feel like and sound like? What would it be like to be with someone who loves you just the way you are?

In this little book I will show you some tools that myself and others have used to bring this about. There are simple processes to follow and you are invited to complete them with a light heart and an open mind. As well as being a manual, this book tells the story of my own journey to finding someone to share my life with. It's meant to be fun and can be used in conjunction with my Meeting Your Perfect Mate workshops. I hope you enjoy it and your own journey to finding that special person.

CHAPTER 1

Writing Goals

♥

Some people create goals for careers, business, finances, renovations and even holidays and achieve great success in these areas but most of us never think of writing down our relationship goals. Isn't that interesting?

Writing Goals

When I first heard about the idea of writing down my goals, I don't think I'd ever written down a goal in my life. I'd heard of successful people setting goals and achieving them but it had never occurred to me to write down my own goals. As I thought about this I realised that it was probably because I hadn't thought about what my goals actually were. (This might explain the lack of direction in my life at the time and the feeling that I wasn't really getting anywhere.) And what if I didn't reach those goals? That would be a disaster, wouldn't it? I mean why go to all that effort when there was no guarantee of a result, right? Wrong! As I have the discovered, the process of finding out what you would like in your life, actually helps bring those things closer to you. I now look at what I would like in every area of my life however when i looked at what I wanted in a relationship, it took me almost two years to figure it out.

Yet again I had met the 'man of my dreams' and as usual it ended after 3 months. The reason this one was particularly harsh was that I had just completed 10 months of counselling and had attended a 3 month intensive personal development seminar. I believed these had

Writing Goals

rendered me completely "cured" of any relationship difficulties and would allow me to sail off into the sunset and live happily ever after with my perfect mate. How naive I was!

While I gained much in the way of healing, insight and relationship skills from counselling and the seminar, there was still something missing. Either I was choosing the wrong type of person or I was just rubbish at relationships. My bets were on the second option.

A friend had suggested a couple of years beforehand, that I write down a description of my ideal man and this would help to bring him into my life. I, of course, dismissed this idea as mumbo jumbo hippie tripe! Constructing some kind of plan in order to meet someone just felt unnatural and contrived to me. So I continued with my current approach. Two years later I still hadn't been able meet someone 'naturally' like 'normal people' and the feeling of failure in this area of my life was beginning to overwhelm me. The idea that you list all the attributes of your ideal partner, read it regularly and then in 6 months to a year's time that person materializes in your life had seemed a little

Writing Goals

farfetched when I first heard it, but now it was starting to look like a good plan because right now, I was all out of options. It was obvious that my current approach wasn't working well - 37 years of age and my longest relationship to date had lasted only 2 ½ years and that was over 10 years before.

What were my choices? I could sit and cry about it and tell myself how flawed I was, running round and round like a little mouse in a wheel or I could give up the last shreds of the idea that life-unfolds-in-a-magical-and-brilliant-way-and-requires-no-real-effort-from-me. I decided that the latter was the most favoured choice - especially after trying the first one and getting nowhere. According to Albert Einstein "The definition of insanity is doing the same thing over and over again and expecting different results". Thinking about this quote, I asked myself if it applied to me and the way I went about choosing my partner. I figured it did and thus I began the task of writing my first goal.

Notes

CHAPTER 2

Getting honest with yourself

Getting honest with yourself

♥

Writing down the truth about what we want in a partner may not be easy because it can bring up our fears and limitations.

Getting honest with yourself

While carrying out this exercise, there was a part of me that thought the whole thing rather frivolous but another part of me was scared. What if I got what I wanted and then discovered it wasn't what I wanted after all? Maybe I liked being single? Of course that scared part was the part of me that liked things to stay the same. Even though I was lonely at times, I made all my own decisions and had full control over my life. If someone came into my life, things would change and I might not like it. I might have to give up my freedom. There were many conflicting thoughts in my head but fortunately the risks were outnumbered by the benefits.

At my first attempt, I produced an extensive list of all the attributes I didn't want e.g. doesn't smoke, isn't married, doesn't watch sports all weekend, doesn't go to the pub every night – this wasn't a very inspiring list. It took some time to turn these around to positive features but even when I did, it still wasn't enough. What I needed was a fuller picture of how life would be with my ideal mate; I needed to bring some feeling into it and to add some colour. Half an hour and a glass of wine later, I had the basis of a short story, including the things we loved to do together, our environment (home, friends etc.) and how we interacted. Things were starting to shape up!

Getting honest with yourself

I read the story every day for about a month, making little changes and gradually refining it until it was just right. For the next three months or so I read it about once a week, then only occasionally. Around 6 months after writing the story, I met the man I came to fall in love with. This was not the type of man I would normally be interested in. He was quiet and shy. I hadn't been very specific in my physical description of my ideal partner, so I didn't recognize him when he showed up.

I first met John at a course we happened to both be attending. The group got together once a week and during this time we interacted on occasion. Once the course finished, a few of us would meet up now and then to discuss our progress. The group slowly dwindled until it was mostly only John and I catching up. It was around this time (about six months after our first meeting) I realised I had fallen for this man and part of me couldn't understand why because he just didn't fit my usual type! This was months after I had stopped reading my story, so when I went back and looked at it, I couldn't believe it; there he was, on the pages of my book! Less than a year after writing the story, I had met and fallen in love with my ideal partner. The good news was that he felt the same about me.

Getting honest with yourself

So, there you have it! That's how I experienced Meeting My Perfect Mate and it's exactly because of this that you now have this book in front of you.

What I would like to do now is to show you in more detail how to make this magic happen. There is however one essential ingredient you'll need to bring to the mix and that is… COMMITMENT! Ooh it's a big scary word for many, right? Might make you want to pull back a bit, be wary? That's ok; you don't have to be afraid; it's only a word. What's more, if you are looking for a relationship, it's a word you might want to make friends with!

How about starting by making a commitment to yourself that you will follow through with this exercise? Who knows, you might even come to like the word! With this in mind, I have created a small declaration for you to read and sign that will assist you in making your commitment more binding.

Getting honest with yourself

Your Commitment

I _____ (Your signature)

commit to carrying out the exercises in this book with joy and purpose!

_____ (Today's date)

So, what do you think, are you ready to do it? Are you ready to choose what you really want? Are you prepared to commit your ideas to paper through a 4 step process? You are?

Great, let's go!

CHAPTER 3

Step 1: Get the Feel

Step 1: Get the Feel

♥

Have you noticed that when things go well for you and you are in good humour, that life is easy and more good things happen?

Step 1: Get the Feel

For example, you get a great parking spot at the shopping centre and then you pick the fastest queue in the supermarket! The flip side of that is when things go wrong. You get out of bed and stub your toe and you get frustrated and then you can't find your car keys, which make you late for work and then everything is just too hard. Can you see the connection here? Happy feelings attract happy thoughts, which mean more happy feelings. Frustrated feelings attract frustrated thoughts, which often means...look out - bad day ahead!

For those of you who are familiar with the belief that the universe sends you what you focus on, you may also know that the more specific you are, the more likely you are to have your desires fulfilled. The bit to remember is that the universe doesn't know the difference between what you want and what you don't want; it works on the basis of bringing you more of the energies or feelings that you are already experiencing. So if you are willing to be the energy of your desire, the universe says "Ok, Elizabeth is emanating a lot of "I am having a fun day" energy, let's send her some more of that!"

Now you have an idea of how your feelings affect you, we can try a little exercise on connecting to different feelings.

Step 1: Get the Feel

Exercise – Choose Your Feelings

Remember a time when you saw or did something that made you happy. For some of us, we may have to go back a bit to find this but it can be anything, from laughing with friends to watching your favourite team winning the final. Once you have that feeling, try to locate the area within your body where it's coming from and if possible expand the feeling. We can call this feeling happiness, joy, love or some other word that works for you.

Now repeat the exercise, only this time, think of a situation where you felt angry, cheated or depressed. Are you able to feel the difference in your body between these two situations? Hopefully you can. If not, repeat the exercise until you get a sense of it. This exercise shows us two things; firstly, you can control your feelings – just not all of the time; and secondly, what we focus on creates our feelings i.e. thought creates feeling. This is the Law of Attraction where your thoughts create your feelings which create your physical experience.

So all you have to do is bring up the energy of what you desire and the universe will provide – amazing!

Step 1: Get the Feel

However what if you get stuck in a feeling of sadness or frustration and you can't get away from it? When we think about our past relationships, joy and happiness are often not the first feelings to surface. We think about all the pain we had and how we don't want to experience that again. It is not easy to jump from sadness to joy, from frustration to optimism. The good news is there is an Emotional Guidance Scale which lists the development of emotion from fear to joy:

Step 1: Get the Feel

Emotional Guidance Scale:

1	Joy/Appreciation/Empowered/Freedom/Love
2	Passion
3	Enthusiasm/Eagerness/Happiness
4	Positive Expectation/Belief
5	Optimism
6	Hopefulness
7	Contentment
8	Boredom
9	Pessimism
10	Frustration/Irritation/Impatience
11	Overwhelmedness
12	Disappointment
13	Doubt
14	Worry
15	Blame
16	Discouragement
17	Anger
18	Revenge
19	Hatred/Rage
20	Jealousy
21	Insecurity/Guilt/Unworthiness
22	Fear/Grief/Depression/Despair/Powerlessness

Step 1: Get the Feel

Exercise - Using the Emotional Guidance Scale (EGS)

Run your eye over the 22 items on the EGS. Now close your eyes and think about which of those emotions you are currently feeling. Take a few moments to do this. The next step is to speak and think yourself up the scale, one emotion at a time. You may even be able to jump up a few emotions at once. Let's say you feel "frustration" (10). To try to jump up to #1 emotion from here could be quite hard, so you might try "pessimism" (9). Stay with this feeling for a while until you really feel it – then climb higher up and so on. Your goal is to be at the top feeling place. Use your past experiences to find the next emotion on the scale.

This is ONLY an emotional/mental exercise to be carried out in a quiet spot and not tried out on those around you. So instead of just saying to yourself "get over it", you are naming your emotions, you are allowing them to be expressed and then you are letting them go, one emotion at a time until you feel better. For more information on this go to: http://mariaerving.com/how-to-use-the-abraham-hicks-emotional-guidance-scale/

Now you have the feel, let's see how we get the look!

Notes

Notes

Notes

CHAPTER 4

Step 2: Get the Look

Step 2: Get the Look

♥

Its now time to decide what you want your perfect mate to look like physically.

Step 2: Get the Look

I know some people will be saying 'Oh but I don't care what they look like, looks are not important to me' and that's fine. However if you had two people in front of you who had all the qualities you are looking for but one had dark hair and the other had blonde, which one would you choose?

One of the key elements of this process is to be specific. So put away those ideas about looks not being important and let your imagination go do its thing. To assist you in this process, I've constructed a table with a number of physical attributes. This is by no means an exhaustive list and I encourage you to go off into fantasy land (or even just your local shopping centre) to get ideas about the physical attributes that you most desire:

Step 2: Get the Look

Area of Interest	Possible Description	Area of Interest	Possible Description
Height	Be specific	Hair	Long, short, curly, thin, fine, thick, blonde, red, brown black, streaked
Build	Big, medium, small, muscular, wiry, slim.	Eyes	Colour, shape, bright, clear, long lashes, crinkly smiling eyes.
Torso	Long, short, smooth, hairy, muscled, tanned	Mouth	Full lips, thin lips, pale lips, creased from smiling.
Chest	Large, medium, small, muscular, wiry, slim.	Ears	Large, small - type of lobes
Skin	Olive, smooth, dark, pale.	Nose	Long short, full, slim, button.
Arms and Legs	Long, short, smooth, hairy, muscled, tanned	Voice	Soft, deep, accent,
Hands	Large, smooth, rough, long nails	Chin	Large, jutting, square, round
Head/face	Large, small, oval, square, facial hair.	Ethnic origins	Asian, European, African.

Step 2: Get the Look

Important!

Be very specific and write a whole page just on physical appearance if you can. The more specific you are, the more chance you have of manifesting what you want.

Notes

Notes

Notes

CHAPTER 5

Step 3: Character Traits

Step 3: Character Traits

♥

Now that you know what they look like, what about how will they interact with you?

Step 3: Character Traits

What would be the ideal? Do you like a lot of physical contact and lots of attention or do you prefer more space and to be the one giving the attention?

We all have our pet hates about past partners or spouses and can list their faults with confidence and ease but what about the good stuff?

Exercise – Get the Vibe

List the character traits you like most in a partner. List them them in the positive. If you find this difficult to do, refer to the table on the next page which has the trait you dislike in the first column and a positive alternative in the second.

You are looking for a minimum of 30 traits but the more you identify, the closer you'll get to what you want.

Step 3: Character Traits

Trait I dislike	Trait I Like
Shopping addict	Spends less than one hour a week shopping
Sports fanatic	Spends less than one hour a week watching sports
Drinks too much	Drinks alcohol moderately or Drinks only alcohol-free beverages
Throws money away	Uses excellent money managing skills
Stingy	Is generous with money
Smokes	Is drug free
Picks their nose	Enjoys good personal hygiene and is considerate of others regarding bodily secretions and expulsions
Watches TV too much	Spends less than 2 hours a week watching TV
Untidy	Is considerate and respectful of my ideas of tidiness and enjoys helping to keep a clean and tidy living space.
Antisocial/ showing off/ boasting	Enjoys a full/moderate/minimal amount of socialising. Is interesting and modest company, has good listening skills, empathetic and a great story teller.

Step 3: Character Traits

Trait I dislike	Trait I Like
Emotionally or Physically Violent	Treats me with respect emotionally and physically at all times
Emotionally disconnected	Interactive and communicates with warmth and ease
Dishonest	Speaks honestly and with thoughtfulness
Indecisive	Makes decisions with ease and consideration
Sarcastic, calls me names, puts me down	Talks to me in a respectful and considerate manner
Bad taste in clothes	Practises good fashion sense and his/her style compliments mine
Doesn't discuss relationship difficulties	Interested in personal growth and development
Infidelity	Is interested in a monogamous relationship
Doesn't feel emotionally attuned	Has a strong emotional connection/balance

Step 3: Character Traits

Here are a few other traits, lifestyle preferences and activities you might like to consider:

More things to consider...

Financially secure/abundant

Family live close/far away

Would like/not like to have children

Has specific ethnic background

Enjoys nature/bush/beach

Enjoys occasional quiet times

Has a sibling around my age

Gets on well with his/her family

Gets on well with children

Has children (children's age?)

Generally gets on well with members of the opposite sex.

Has a strong religious/spiritual conviction

Has similar or matching values to your own

Step 3: Character Traits

Reach For the Stars

If you find that you come up with an idea and then decide that you couldn't possibly have it, stop there - this is just a limiting belief, it is not the truth. The only limitation we have is our imagination, so go for gold. A friend of mine decided she would love to have a motor home and a boat and added these to her list of desires. Also, she has sleep apnoea and has to wear a mask strapped over her nose and mouth which connects to an air blowing machine via a tube and runs all night long. In her list of attributes she wrote something like "(my perfect mate) is happy to sleep with a woman who wears a respiratory device in bed". And guess what, this friend, got it all! When asked after their first night together if the machine was a distraction, her new mate replied that due to mild tinnitus he found the buzzing of the machine rather soothing!

Notes

Notes

Notes

CHAPTER 6

Step 4: Get the Experience

Step 4: Get the Experience

♥

What we want to do now is to create the type of experience you would like to have with your ideal partner.

Step 4: Get the Experience

To ensure you get all the details you need for this part of the exercise; it helps to write this as a story about the perfect day together. As you write your story, weave in as many of the physical characteristics and traits you have on your list. Write it in the present moment and as though you are already in a loving relationship with this person.

Important! Ensure that you write the story using positive language. Be sure to write only what you want and not what you don't want. When we say "don't forget your keys" or "I can't be late", our subconscious mind hears "forget your keys" or "be late" because it doesn't process negatives. So check regularly for this type of language. If you find this difficult, try thinking about what you don't want and then think what the opposite of that might be.

Words to avoid: always, never, doesn't, should, shouldn't, couldn't, isn't, can't, won't, will be, was and wasn't.

Remember! Be very specific. Think about ex-spouses, dependent children, child support and crazy in-laws. The more specific you are, the more chance you have of manifesting what you want.

Step 4: Get the Experience

Have a look at these examples:

Waking up

1. Tom woke me this morning with a gentle kiss. He looked into my eyes as he stroked my hair with his strong, soft hand and told me how beautiful I was.

2. Carol woke me this morning with a warm cuddle and a sleepy "Good morning my love"

3. Derek woke me with a steaming hot cup of coffee, a perfect dew covered rose and the morning papers.

4. Sam woke me nice and early this morning to catch the sunrise and have an invigorating jog along the beach.

What's it for you? What's your favourite way to be woken in the morning? Do you like breakfast in bed? Do you like to go for a jog? Is it croissants and coffee? Do you like to snuggle or make love?

What would you like to do on this wonderful day together? What gives you that yummy feeling?

Step 4: Get the Experience

Scenario 1 – It's a sunny day and you decide to go to the beach. How do you get there? What do you take? Will you play games on the beach? What type of a beach is it? Is it busy or deserted? Did you bring a picnic or will you have lunch at that nice restaurant overlooking the ocean? What are you/your partner wearing? How do they smell? What can you see, hear and smell at the beach? What do you say to each other? How does your partner act toward you?

Scenario 2 – It's raining and you stay in all day making love. Do you stroke and cuddle each other? Give each other a massage? Is your love-making gentle or energetic? How do they hold you? Are there lots of pillows and soft blankets? What do your surroundings look like? Can you hear the rain? What are you feeling? What do they say to you? Can you smell sweet or spicy perfumes or oils? Is there music playing? Do you dance or play games?

Other ideas might be: You go to see your favourite band or musician or show. Maybe you go to car racing, horse riding or take a trip to the mountains for a trek or snow skiing. Perhaps you would like to get dressed up and go to a fabulous ball! Perhaps you are having a naked candlelit picnic on the living room floor. There are no limits to what

Step 4: Get the Experience

your imagination can create, however I suggest you keep within the realms of reality. To wake up and suddenly you are the Prince/Queen of Denmark with serfs and a castle is probably a little farfetched for most of us!

These are just a few ideas to get you started. You can have a quiet, relaxed day if that's your thing or an energetic day where you combine a few activities.

The main thing is to get the senses involved because we live through our senses. What you see, smell, touch, feel, hear and taste are key elements in creating a memorable day.

Step 4: Get the Experience

Where, When and How

There are a couple of ways to complete this exercise, depending on how your mind works. For some people, a few days is required to mull things over and allow their images to emerge slowly. For others, it's get straight onto the computer and start writing. You may want to watch some movies or read a book that represents your ideal day. Whichever way you decide to do this, give yourself the time and space to make it an enjoyable experience and not a chore.

To help you get focussed on what you want, here are a couple of ideas.

1. Make a date with yourself. Go to your calendar and pencil in a special time for you. E.g.
   Date: Saturday 27th October
   Time: 1pm
   Place: my place
   Reason: My ideal day

2. Allow yourself a few hours without interruptions.

Step 4: Get the Experience

3. Take the phone off the hook

4. Put on some music to help create your desired mood

5. Wear clothes that represent the kind of day you would like

6. Burn some pleasant smelling oils

7. Get a glass of your favourite hot or cold drink;

8. Find a comfortable spot to write - computer, the kitchen table or sitting on your bed. If your perfect day was at the beach, you may want to go the beach and do it.

For the best results, I highly recommend you complete this task in a single sitting. If you don't, you may find yourself making excuses not to complete it and then it's likely to slowly fade away with all those other great ideas you had.

Just for you
just for fun
not to tell anyone!

Step 4: Get the Experience

Important!

I recommend you don't tell your friends or family you are doing this. Even though these people may have your best interests at heart, they sometimes unwittingly put a damper on things. If they are anything like my family they might say something like:

'That's silly, you'll never meet anyone sitting at home writing, just go out and meet someone nice' or 'Stop being so serious about it, just chill out and it will all happen naturally' or

'I know this really nice single guy/girl at work and I'm sure you two would get on really well'

I am sure there is an element of truth in each of the above statements but it is also true that increasing the odds improves our chances of success. We sometimes can't help being influenced by other people's points of view and this distracts us from where we want to go. Even though advice from friends or family is well intended it isn't always helpful. Have you ever been really excited about something and told a friend only to have them burst your bubble? Sharing can diminish our excitement about what we are trying to achieve so remember: Just for me just for fun not to tell anyone!

Step 4: Get the Experience

Guidelines for Reading Your Story

Read your story every day for the first couple of weeks and at least three times a week for the next three to six months. As you do this, refine any aspects, experiences or details to help make it spectacularly real for you. To get the most from this, it's beneficial to allow yourself to feel what it's like to be with that person. As you read, imagine yourself there, experiencing the delights of spending time with this lovely person, knowing that they totally accept and love you.

This is a guide only, but from my own experience, the more you read it, the more apparent your inner desires become, giving you insight into what makes you happy.

To add extra power to this technique, you can use the process called Vibrosonics developed by Michael Domeyko Rowland. Before going to sleep at night, run your 'perfect day' in your head like a little film clip. For optimum results, do this for one or two minutes at a time but you can start with maybe 30 seconds and then build from there.

Step 4: Get the Experience

Note: If you start to run the story and you get sidetracked or negative feelings or images emerge, stop, open your eyes, acknowledge them and then let them go. Once you feel you have released those unhelpful feelings or images, start again.

While this technique may take time to master, the results are amazing. It may sound like a difficult thing to do ... but if you stop and think about it, you are already doing it, the only difference is that you are currently running a movie that is not giving you what you want.

Notes

Notes

Notes

Notes

CHAPTER 7

Final Note

Final Note

♥

This is as far as I can accompany you along your journey.

Final Note

I hope you have enjoyed the journey and I wish you all the best in bringing your dreams to life.

Here are 10 prompts to assist you in completing your story:

1. Be clear about what you want – what you focus on will come to you
2. Add a little extra – reach for the stars
3. Add action – this will help to guide your unconscious mind
4. Use positive language – the subconscious doesn't process negatives
5. Position yourself in the story – tell the story as though you are right there
6. Use colour – you can add some images to your story to give it more depth
7. Smell the roses – remember your olfactory system is a powerful tool in invoking feeling
8. Follow the steps – read and adjust your story till it feels right
9. Call to action – start today, you've waited long enough to fulfil your desires!
10. Joie de vivre – enjoy the story, remember to add the fun stuff!

ABOUT THE AUTHOR

Elizabeth is a qualified relationship counsellor and energy worker. She has been exploring relationships and how they work for over 25 years. Elizabeth is an accredited facilitator in Communication and Personal Awareness and a Master Practitioner in NLP and EFT.

Meet Your Perfect Mate is her first book and she is already busy working on her second. Born in Glasgow, Scotland, Elizabeth currently resides in Perth, Western Australia.

THANKS

My deepest thanks to all my friends who have helped me to get this book to its completed format. Special mention for Katie Pelosi, my graphic designer, to Karen at Serenity Press for being the catalyst and to Caroline Crosbie for her honest feedback and continued support.

TESTIMONIALS

"My whole life I had picked the wrong guys following a similar track each time. I read Elizabeth's book and decided to put it into practice. First writing a list of exactly everything I wanted in a guy, making sure I had every little detail. Shortly after reading this book I met my perfect mate. He was different to someone I was generally attracted to, but I realised that he was everything I had put on my list. Six and a half years later and we are happily married with three beautiful girls. Without Elizabeth's book I would have never broke the pattern of falling for guys that were not everything I wanted and would never have had my dream come true. I highly recommend this book to everyone.

– Sam

Some 8 years ago, I had the great fortune to read and use 'How to meet your prefect mate'. I thought about and wrote down what I wanted in a perfect partner, his physical looks, personality and spirit. Nine months down the line I met my now husband, Cesar. It was incredible how similar he was to my description. I am very grateful to Elizabeth for gifting her book as I believe it played a huge role in my meeting Cesar.

– Jen

TESTIMONIALS

I read Elizabeth's book and felt I had suddenly been given permission to imagine my wildest dreams. I didn't even realise till then how I had never really thought about what I really wanted and why it was important to me. The book made sense on every level and was full of practical easy to follow activities. If you've read about the Law of Attraction and follow what the latest in neuroscience is suggesting you will totally love this simple guide to getting what you want.

– Louise

RECOMMENDED READING

Here are a few websites I would recommend:

– carolinecrosbie.com

– accessconsciousness.com

– www.successlovefreedom.com

www.ingramcontent.com/pod-product-compliance
Lightning Source LLC
Chambersburg PA
CBHW042345300426
44110CB00029B/31